Crafts for Kids Who Are Wild About

Deserts

Crafts for Kids Who Are
WILD
ABOUT
DESERTS

By Kathy Ross
Illustrated by Sharon Lane Holm

The Millbrook Press   Brookfield, Connecticut

For my friend Missy, who is pretty good at identifying my projects—K.R.

For my dear friend, Kim—S.L.H.

Library of Congress Cataloging-in-Publication Data
Ross, Kathy (Katharine Reynolds), 1948–
Crafts for kids who are wild about deserts / Kathy Ross ; illustrated by Sharon Lane Holm.
p. cm.
Includes bibliographical references.
Summary: Provides instructions for twenty projects, creating such things as a cactus puppet,
tortoise treasure keeper, egg carton rattlesnake, oasis stamp licker, sand art necklace, and more.

ISBN 0-7613-0954-3 (lib. bdg.)
1. Handicraft—Juvenile literature. 2. Desert animals in art—Juvenile literature.
[1. Handicraft. 2. Deserts in art.] I. Holm, Sharon Lane, ill. II. Title.
TT160.R7142   1998
745.5—dc21   97-47093   CIP   AC

Published by The Millbrook Press, Inc.
2 Old New Milford Road
Brookfield, Connecticut 06804

Contents

Introduction   7

Expanding Cactus Puppet   8

Cactus Table Decoration   10

Wolf Spider   12

Green Toad Paperweight   14

Tortoise Treasure Keeper   16

Egg Carton Rattlesnake   18

Palmate Gecko Magnet   20

Pecking Woodpecker   22

Elf Owl Puppet   24

Lappet-faced Vulture Puppet   26

Bottle Peccary   28

Fennec Face Mask   30

Bactrian Camel Puppet   32

Squirting Spotted Skunk   34

Jackrabbit Marionette   36

Envelopes Camel Puppet   39

Plate Gerbil   40

Coyote Paper Keeper   42

Oasis Stamp Licker   44

Sand Art Necklace   46

Books About Deserts   48

Introduction

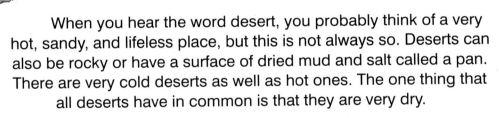

When you hear the word desert, you probably think of a very hot, sandy, and lifeless place, but this is not always so. Deserts can also be rocky or have a surface of dried mud and salt called a pan. There are very cold deserts as well as hot ones. The one thing that all deserts have in common is that they are very dry.

Desert areas not only get little rainfall, under 10 inches (25 cm) per year, but also have a rapid evaporation rate due to strong winds and minimal cloud coverage.

Knowing all this, it is remarkable that we find such an astounding variety of plant and animal life thriving in the desert climate, as well as a large number of people. I hope the projects in this book will inspire you to find out more about the fascinating life-forms found in the deserts.

Kathy Ross

Expanding Cactus Puppet

Here is what you need:

water
plastic margarine tub
teaspoon
green food coloring
adult-size sock with a ribbed cuff
Styrofoam tray for drying
small round oatmeal box
scissors
white tissue paper
yellow tissue paper
white glue

Here is what you do:

Put ½ cup (118 ml) of water in the plastic tub. Color the water with a teaspoon of green food coloring. Hold the sock by the toe and dip it into the green water to dye the sock. The sock will suck up most of the colored water. Squeeze out the excess green water and put the sock on the Styrofoam tray to dry.

After it has dried, turn the sock inside out. Tie the foot into a knot. Turn the sock right side out again so the toe now forms the rounded top of the cactus.

The pleated covering of the saguaro cactus allows the plant to expand as it stores water during wet periods.

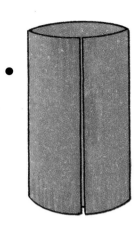

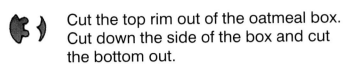 Cut the top rim out of the oatmeal box. Cut down the side of the box and cut the bottom out.

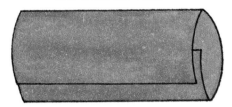

Wrap the sides of the box around itself to make a small tube. Put the tube inside the cuff of the sock to form the stem of the cactus.

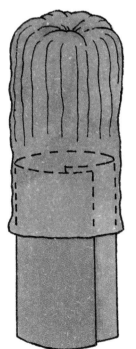

Cut the flowers for the cactus from the white tissue paper. Cut a center for each flower from the yellow tissue paper. Glue the flowers to the top of the cactus.

To expand the cactus, just put your hand inside the puppet and push out on the cardboard. The pleats in the cactus will stretch out just the way a real cactus does when it absorbs water in the desert.

Cactus Table Decoration

Here is what you need:

pencil
clear disposable plastic cup
cereal-box cardboard
scissors
white glue
sand
Styrofoam tray for drying
eight burdocks*
green poster paint
paintbrush
disposable plastic tub
masking tape

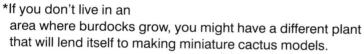

*If you don't live in an
area where burdocks grow, you might have a different plant
that will lend itself to making miniature cactus models.

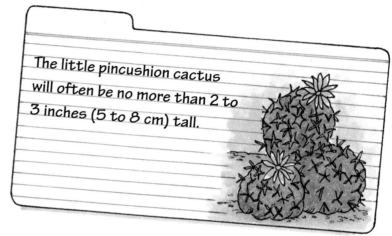

The little pincushion cactus will often be no more than 2 to 3 inches (5 to 8 cm) tall.

Here is what you do:

Trace around the rim of the cup on the cardboard. Cut the circle out.

Cover the plain side of the cardboard with glue, and then sprinkle sand on the glue. Let the sand-covered circle dry completely on the Styrofoam tray.

Stick the burdocks together in two groups of four each to look like cactus. Use the green paint to color them. Let the burdocks dry on the Styrofoam tray.

 Glue the burdocks on the sand-covered circle to look like cactus in the desert.

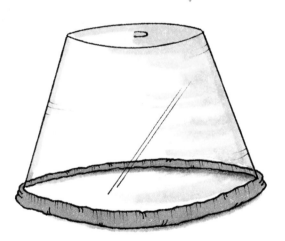

Cover the rim of the cup with the masking tape to create a better gluing surface. Dip the tape-covered rim in glue, then place it over the desert scene. Let the project dry completely on the Styrofoam tray.

You might want to make your cactus "in bloom" by adding small tissue flowers.

Wolf Spider

Here is what you need:

old black knit glove
scissors
cotton balls
white glue
1-inch (2.5-cm) Styrofoam ball
eight twist ties
black poster paint
paintbrush
disposable plastic tub
eight peppercorns

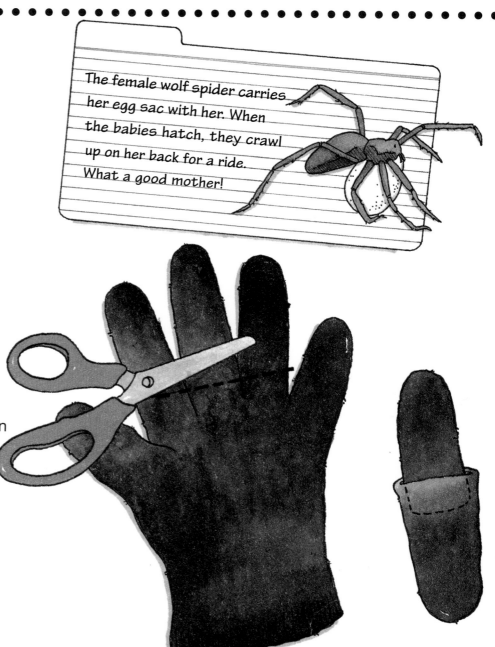

The female wolf spider carries her egg sac with her. When the babies hatch, they crawl up on her back for a ride. What a good mother!

Here is what you do:

Cut the two longest fingers from the glove. Stuff the two fingers with cotton balls to just hold the shape of the fingers. Slide the open end of one finger over the other to form the body of the spider. Attach the glove fingers together with glue.

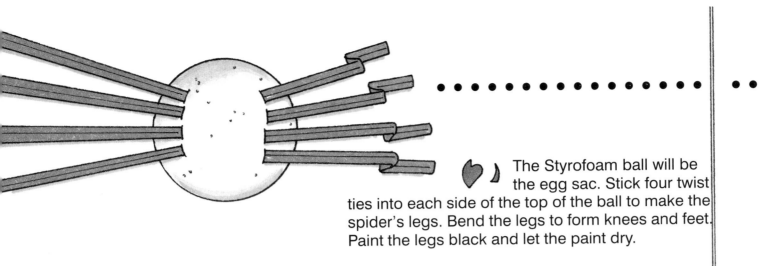

The Styrofoam ball will be the egg sac. Stick four twist ties into each side of the top of the ball to make the spider's legs. Bend the legs to form knees and feet. Paint the legs black and let the paint dry.

Glue the body of the spider over the top of the egg sac and the legs.

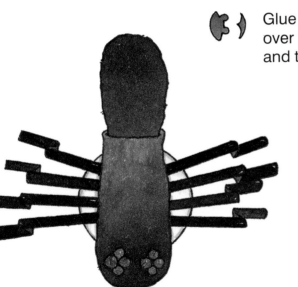

Glue eight peppercorns to the head of the spider for the eyes.

You might want to glue a string to the back of the spider for a dragline, so you can hang it from a wall.

13

Green Toad Paperweight

Here is what you need:

two 1-inch (2.5-cm) wooden craft beads
white glue
flat rock about 4 by 3 inches (10 by 8 cm)
fourteen ½-inch (1-cm) wooden craft beads
water
plastic margarine tub
brown poster paint
paintbrush
old white sock
scissors
green poster paint
Styrofoam tray for drying
green marker
black marker

The bumps of a green toad secrete a slimy mucus that helps keep the toad moist in the dry desert climate.

Here is what you do:

Glue the two larger beads along the edge at one end of the top of the rock to form eyes for the toad.

Glue the smaller beads all over the top of the rock to form the bumps on the back of the toad. Let the glue dry before continuing with this project.

Mix one part water to two parts glue in the plastic tub. Add a small amount of brown paint to the glue to turn it a tan shade.

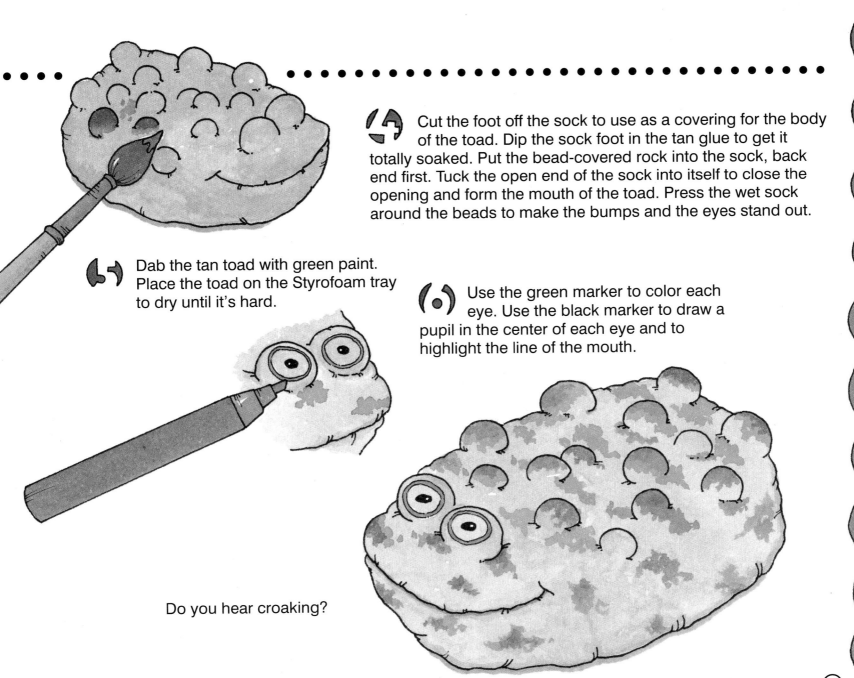

4 Cut the foot off the sock to use as a covering for the body of the toad. Dip the sock foot in the tan glue to get it totally soaked. Put the bead-covered rock into the sock, back end first. Tuck the open end of the sock into itself to close the opening and form the mouth of the toad. Press the wet sock around the beads to make the bumps and the eyes stand out.

5 Dab the tan toad with green paint. Place the toad on the Styrofoam tray to dry until it's hard.

6 Use the green marker to color each eye. Use the black marker to draw a pupil in the center of each eye and to highlight the line of the mouth.

Do you hear croaking?

Tortoise Treasure Keeper

Here is what you need:

small tuna-fish-type can
masking tape
yellow-colored craft glue
about twenty-five buttons in shades of brown
corrugated cardboard
pen
felt
scissors
jar lid small enough to fit under the can
white glue

The slow-moving tortoise can go for long periods of time in the desert without eating or drinking.

Here is what you do:

Invert the can to form a shell for the tortoise. Cover the bottom of the can (now the top of the tortoise shell) with masking tape to create a better gluing surface.

Cover the masking tape with the yellow glue. Arrange as many buttons as you need on top of the glue to cover the top of the tortoise shell.

Place the can on the corrugated cardboard. Sketch the head, legs, and tail of a tortoise coming out from the shell. Cut the tortoise shape out.

Cut a circle of felt to fit inside the jar lid. Put a piece of masking tape in the lid and on one side of the felt circle to create better gluing surfaces. Glue the felt inside the lid, tape side down, with the white glue.

Put a piece of tape on the outside (top) of the lid. Use the white glue to attach the lid to the center of the tortoise shape for a little dish in which to keep small treasures.

Use white glue to attach two buttons to the head of the tortoise for eyes.

Put your tiny treasures in the felt-lined lid and cover them with the can shell of the tortoise to hide them. No one will ever suspect your tortoise has a secret compartment!

Egg Carton Rattlesnake

Here is what you need:

three cardboard egg cartons
scissors
three paper fasteners
brown pipe cleaner
brown poster paint
paintbrush
black poster paint
white poster paint
newspaper to work on

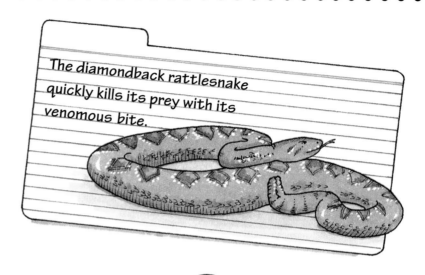

The diamondback rattlesnake quickly kills its prey with its venomous bite.

Here is what you do:

 Cut four strips of four connected egg cups.

Set the egg cup at the end of one strip over the egg cup at the end of a second strip. Push a paper fastener through the top of the two cups to hold them together. Attach the four sections together in a row with the paper fasteners to make the body of the snake.

 Cut eight individual cups from the remaining egg carton.

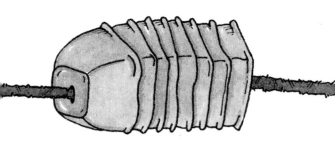

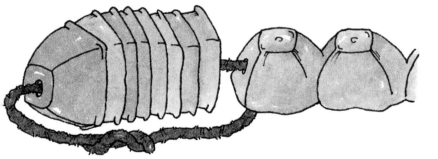

Poke a hole through the bottom of each egg cup.

String the egg cups onto the pipe cleaner to make the rattle for the snake.

Poke a hole at the back of the last egg cup of the snake body. Thread one end of the pipe cleaner with the cups strung on it through the hole. Bring the end of the pipe cleaner down under the cup and back out the end of the snake. Wrap the end of the pipe cleaner around the other end to hold the cups of the rattle in place.

Paint the snake body and the rattle brown. Use the black and white paint to give the snake a diamond pattern on its back. On the first egg cup, use the black paint to mark the snake's eyes and mouth.

You had better not leave this snake around to surprise anyone! The diamondback rattlesnake is considered one of the most dangerous snakes in North America.

Palmate Gecko Magnet

Here is what you need:

two 12-inch (30-cm) brown pipe cleaners
ruler
scissors
white glue
wooden ice-cream spoon
masking tape
Styrofoam tray for drying
facial tissue
yellow-colored glue
sticky-back magnet strip
brown marker
two small black beads

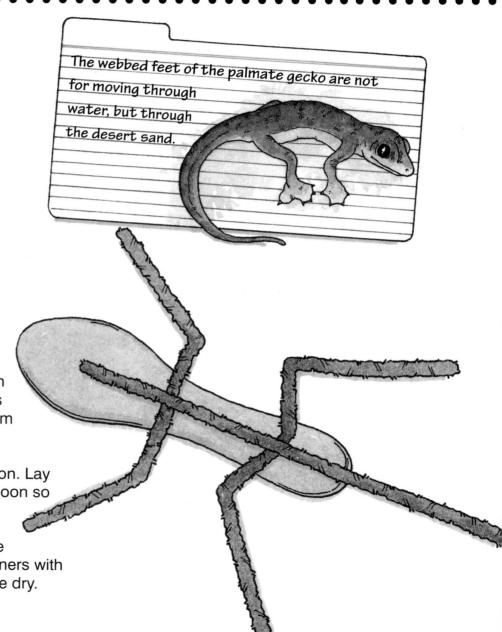

The webbed feet of the palmate gecko are not for moving through water, but through the desert sand.

Here is what you do:

Cut one of the brown pipe cleaners in half to use for the front and back legs of the gecko. Cut a 4-inch (10-cm) piece from the second pipe cleaner for the tail.

Rub glue all over one side of the spoon. Lay the front and back legs across the spoon so that they stick out on each side. Lay the tail along the spoon so that it sticks out the small handle end of the spoon, which will be the back of the gecko. Secure the pipe cleaners with more glue and masking tape and let the glue dry.

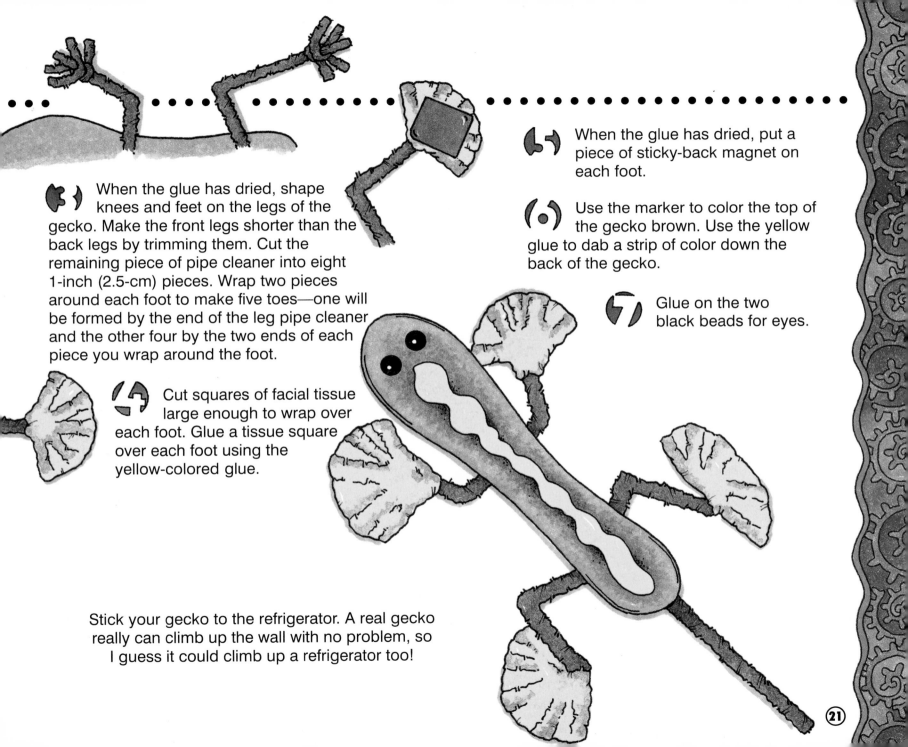

When the glue has dried, shape knees and feet on the legs of the gecko. Make the front legs shorter than the back legs by trimming them. Cut the remaining piece of pipe cleaner into eight 1-inch (2.5-cm) pieces. Wrap two pieces around each foot to make five toes—one will be formed by the end of the leg pipe cleaner and the other four by the two ends of each piece you wrap around the foot.

Cut squares of facial tissue large enough to wrap over each foot. Glue a tissue square over each foot using the yellow-colored glue.

When the glue has dried, put a piece of sticky-back magnet on each foot.

Use the marker to color the top of the gecko brown. Use the yellow glue to dab a strip of color down the back of the gecko.

Glue on the two black beads for eyes.

Stick your gecko to the refrigerator. A real gecko really can climb up the wall with no problem, so I guess it could climb up a refrigerator too!

Pecking Woodpecker

Here is what you need:

ruler
markers
white construction paper
scissors
12-inch by 12-inch (30-cm) square of corrugated
    cardboard
green poster paint
paintbrush
paper fastener
stapler
white glue
uncooked brown rice

The gila woodpecker likes to make its home in the saguaro cactus.

Here is what you do:

Use the markers to draw a 3-inch (8-cm)-high gila woodpecker on the white construction paper. Cut the bird out.

To make the cactus, paint half of the bumpy side of the corrugated cardboard green.

Cut a hole in the center of the green-painted section of the cardboard that is about 3 inches (8 cm) high and 2 inches (5 cm) wide.

 Attach the bird to the bottom side of the hole with a paper fastener so that it can move back and forth like it is pecking the hole in the cactus.

Roll the cardboard into a cactus shape with the green on the outside and the brown part showing through the hole to look like the inside of the cactus. Staple the ends at the top and the bottom to hold them in place.

Paint the cactus with white glue and sprinkle it with brown rice to look like the spines of the cactus.

The sharp spines of the cactus keep the gila woodpecker safe from predators.

Elf Owl Puppet

Here is what you need:

green poster paint
paintbrush
12-inch by 12-inch (30-cm) square of
    corrugated cardboard
ruler
scissors
stapler
brown sock
yellow and black construction paper
    scraps
white glue
orange construction paper scraps

The tiny elf owl also likes to make its home in the saguaro cactus.

Here is what you do:

 Paint the bumpy side of the corrugated cardboard green for the outside of the cactus.

When the paint has dried, cut a 3-inch by 4-inch (8-cm by 10-cm) hole in the center of the cardboard. Fold the cardboard into a cylinder shape and staple the ends to hold them in place.

Cut the foot off the brown sock. This will be the owl puppet.

Cut eyes for the owl from the yellow and black paper. Glue the eyes on one side of the sock owl. Cut a beak from orange paper and glue it in place below the eyes.

Put the owl up inside the cactus so that it is looking out the hole. Staple the bottom front of the sock owl to the base of the cactus.

To use your owl puppet, just put your hand up inside the sock and make the owl's head stick out of the cactus as if it is having a look around.

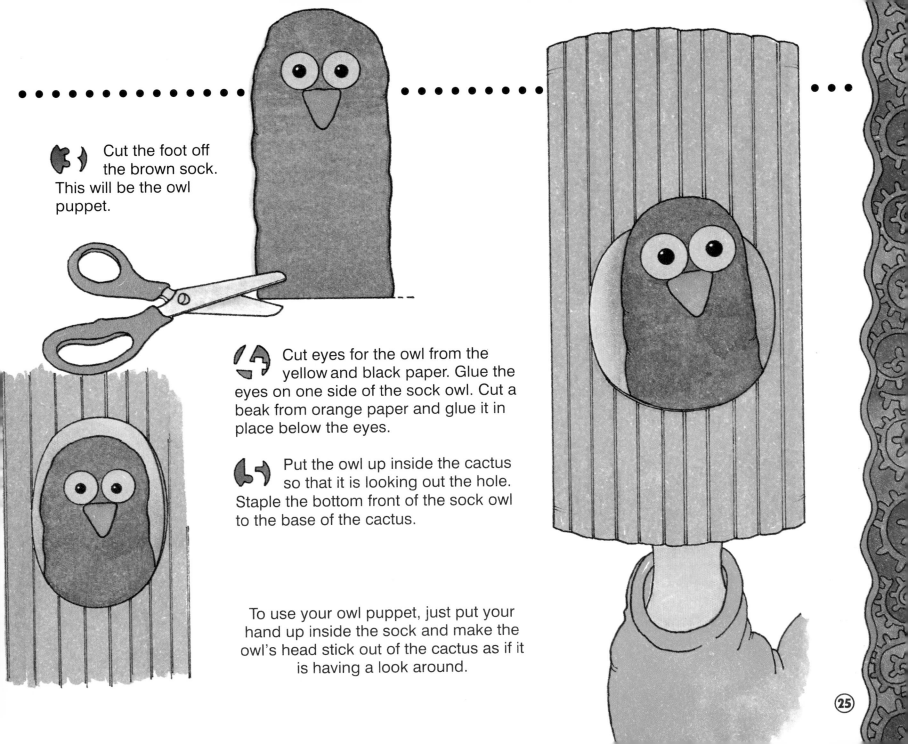

Lappet-faced Vulture Puppet

Here is what you need:

newspaper to work on
black poster paint
paintbrush
four 9-inch (23-cm) uncoated paper
    plates
scissors
red construction paper
black marker
yellow construction paper
white glue
stapler
12-inch (30-cm) black pipe cleaner

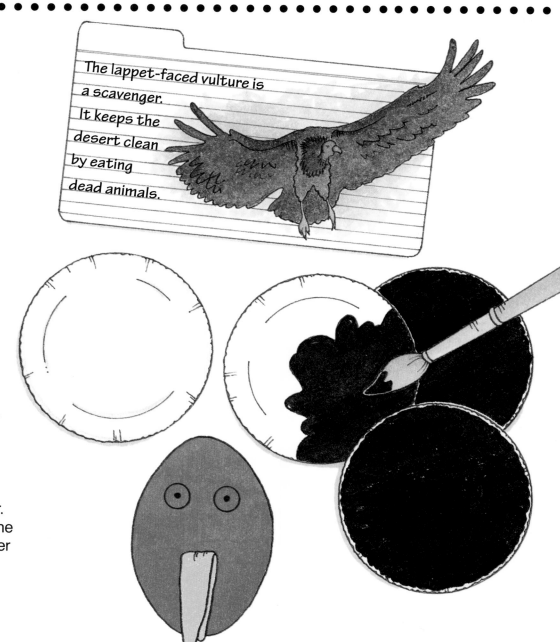

The lappet-faced vulture is a scavenger. It keeps the desert clean by eating dead animals.

Here is what you do:

Paint the bottom side of three of the paper plates black. Let the plates dry.

Cut an oval-shaped head for the vulture from the red paper. Use the marker to draw two eyes on the head. Cut a beak from the yellow paper and glue it in place below the eyes.

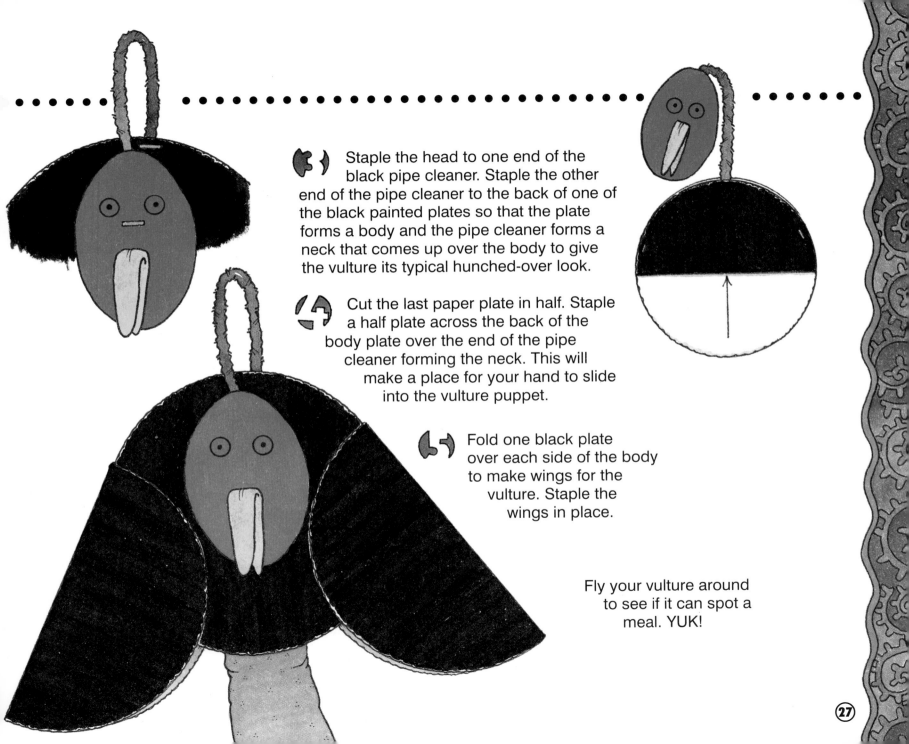

Staple the head to one end of the black pipe cleaner. Staple the other end of the pipe cleaner to the back of one of the black painted plates so that the plate forms a body and the pipe cleaner forms a neck that comes up over the body to give the vulture its typical hunched-over look.

Cut the last paper plate in half. Staple a half plate across the back of the body plate over the end of the pipe cleaner forming the neck. This will make a place for your hand to slide into the vulture puppet.

Fold one black plate over each side of the body to make wings for the vulture. Staple the wings in place.

Fly your vulture around to see if it can spot a meal. YUK!

Bottle Peccary

Here is what you need:

scissors
pair of dark brown or black panty hose
gallon-size bleach bottle, thoroughly
   washed and dried
fiberfill
ruler
blue glue gel
masking tape
two flat black buttons
four yellow map pins
four corks that are the same height

The peccary likes to dine on cactus, including the spines!

Here is what you do:

Cut one leg off the panty hose. Cut off the foot and knot one of the open ends to close it.

Put the bleach bottle, bottom end first, with the lid screwed on, all the way into the stocking. Stuff the fiberfill under the open end of the handle to fill in the space. Knot the open end of the panty hose over the lid of the bottle to hold the fiberfill in place. Trim off any extra stocking.

Cut the second leg off the panty hose. Cut off the foot and knot one end of the stocking to close it. Trim off any extra stocking.

Put the covered bottle into the stocking, lid end first.

Knot the open end of the stocking at the bottom center of the bottle. Trim the excess stocking leaving about 3 inches (7½ cm) for the peccary's tail.

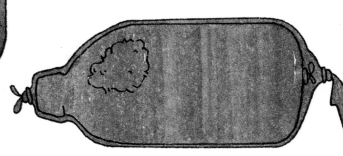

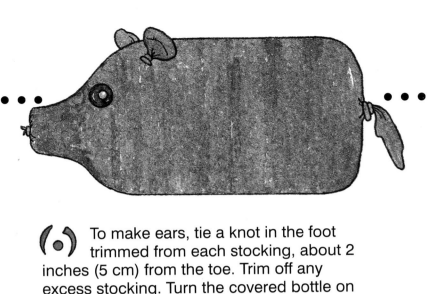

(7) Put a small piece of masking tape on the back of each button to make a better gluing surface. Glue a button about halfway down and on each side of the handle. Put a yellow map pin through one end of the holes in each button to make a pupil.

(6) To make ears, tie a knot in the foot trimmed from each stocking, about 2 inches (5 cm) from the toe. Trim off any excess stocking. Turn the covered bottle on its side with the handle on top. Glue an ear on each side of the handle.

(8) Dip the other two map pins in glue and slip them into the stocking and fiberfill at the lid end of the handle to make the nostrils.

(9) Glue the corks on the bottom of the peccary (the side of the bottle) for legs.

Keep a close eye on this fellow. Within hours of being born, a peccary can outrun a person!

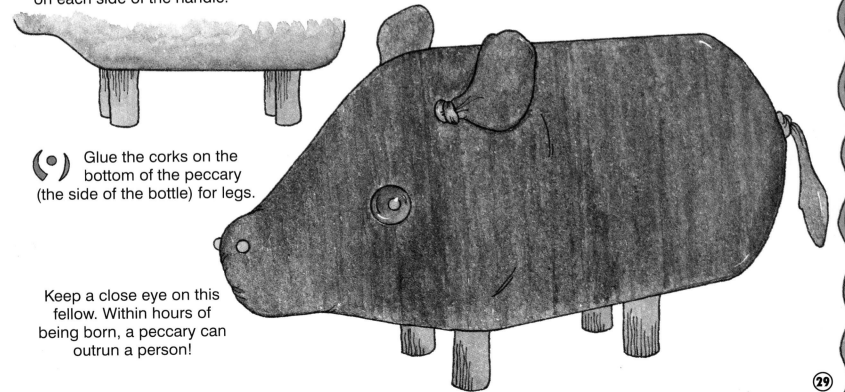

Fennec Face Mask

Here is what you need:

three 9-inch (23-cm) paper plates
scissors
ruler
stapler
newspaper to work on
tan paint
paintbrush
black construction paper scrap
black yarn
white glue
hole punch

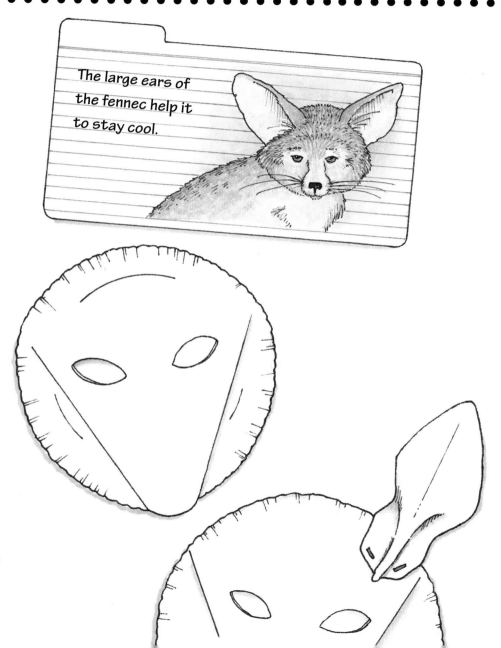

The large ears of the fennec help it to stay cool.

Here is what you do:

Fold the bottom sides of one of the plates in to form a pointed nose for the fennec. Cut two narrow, slightly slanted eyeholes in the mask.

Cut an ear from each of the other two plates that is about 4 inches (10 cm) wide at the base and tapers to a point at the opposite end of the plate.

Fold the base of each ear to give it dimension, then staple the ears to the top of the face mask.

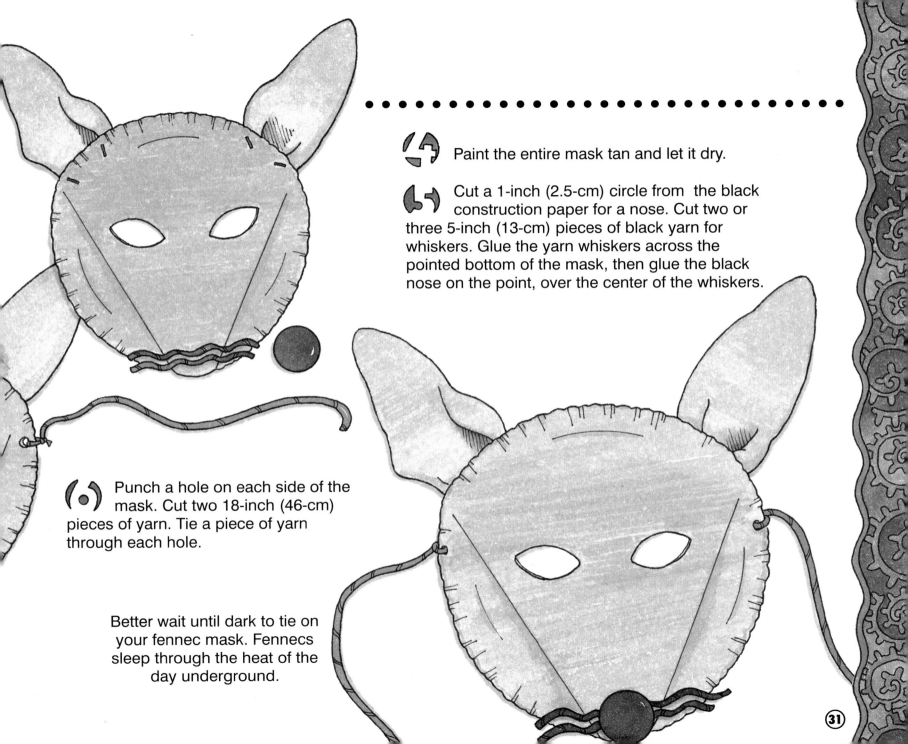

4 Paint the entire mask tan and let it dry.

5 Cut a 1-inch (2.5-cm) circle from the black construction paper for a nose. Cut two or three 5-inch (13-cm) pieces of black yarn for whiskers. Glue the yarn whiskers across the pointed bottom of the mask, then glue the black nose on the point, over the center of the whiskers.

6 Punch a hole on each side of the mask. Cut two 18-inch (46-cm) pieces of yarn. Tie a piece of yarn through each hole.

Better wait until dark to tie on your fennec mask. Fennecs sleep through the heat of the day underground.

31

Bactrian Camel Puppet

Here is what you need:

newspaper to work on
two 9-inch (23-cm) paper plates
brown paint
paintbrush
two brown socks
scissors
fiberfill
stapler
brown construction paper
white glue
black marker
pipe cleaner

The Bactrian camel has two humps in which to store fat for energy. When the fat is used up, the hump will flop to one side.

Here is what you do:

Paint the bottom of both plates brown. Let the paint dry.

Cut off about half of the foot of each sock. The toe ends will be the two humps of the camel. Stuff the two humps with some fiberfill to make them stand up.

Staple one side of the open end of the two sock humps, side by side to the edge of the white side of one of the plates. Do not staple the opening of the humps shut.

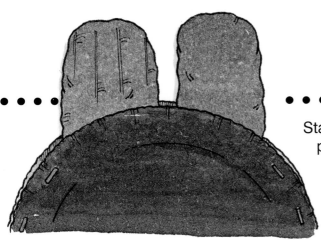

Staple the second plate over the first plate, brown side up, putting the staples on each side of the two humps only.

Cut four legs for the camel from the brown construction paper. Glue two legs on each side of the bottom edge of the camel.

Cut a head and two ears for the camel from the brown construction paper. Glue the ears to the top of the head. Use the black marker to give the camel a face. Staple the head between the two plates on one side of the camel.

Fold the pipe cleaner in half and twist it to make a tail. Spread out the two ends of the pipe cleaner to make the tassel at the end of the tail. Staple the tail between the two plates on the opposite side that the head is on.

To use the camel puppet, put your hand up between the paper plates at the bottom of the camel. After a long journey, deflate one or both humps by pulling out the fiberfill so that the hump falls to one side. Feed the camel and fill the hump with "fat" again for another journey.

Squirting Spotted Skunk

Here is what you need:

scissors
black construction paper
yellow construction paper
paper fastener
white glue
small pink pom-pom
two black beads
fiberfill

The spotted skunk defends itself by squirting a smelly liquid from glands under its tail.

Here is what you do:

Cut an oval shape from the black paper for the body of the skunk. Cut a narrower oval shape for the tail, at least as long as the body. Cut a round head, two small pointed ears, and front and back legs for the skunk.

Cut a spray out of the yellow construction paper that is small enough to be concealed by the tail.

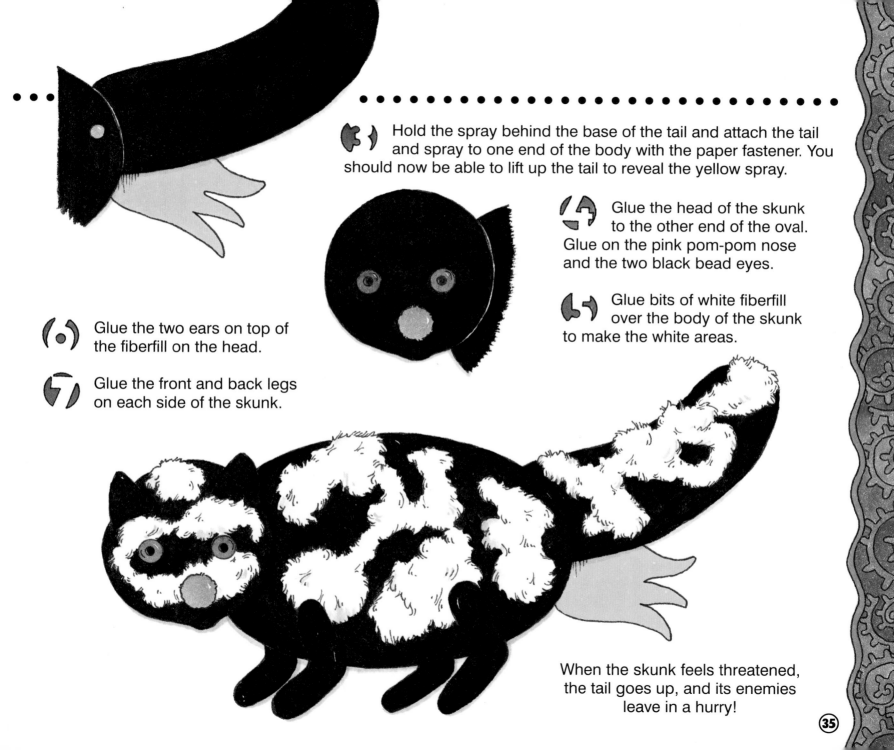

Hold the spray behind the base of the tail and attach the tail and spray to one end of the body with the paper fastener. You should now be able to lift up the tail to reveal the yellow spray.

Glue the head of the skunk to the other end of the oval. Glue on the pink pom-pom nose and the two black bead eyes.

Glue bits of white fiberfill over the body of the skunk to make the white areas.

Glue the two ears on top of the fiberfill on the head.

Glue the front and back legs on each side of the skunk.

When the skunk feels threatened, the tail goes up, and its enemies leave in a hurry!

Jackrabbit Marionette

Here is what you need:

four paper-towel tubes
stapler
ruler
scissors
masking tape
cereal-box cardboard
white glue
pink poster paint
paintbrush
brown poster paint
newspaper to work on
1½ to 2-inch (4- to 5-cm) large black
    pom-pom
two wiggle eyes
fiberfill
yarn
hole punch
toilet-tissue tube

The large feet of the jackrabbit enable it to run very fast.

Here is what you do:

To make each ear, flatten a paper-towel tube and fold the sides of one end inside itself to make the pointed top of the ear. Fold the bottom of the tube in half to give the ear dimension. Staple the bottom to hold the fold in place.

Cut an 8-inch (20-cm) slit up each side of another paper-towel tube and cut across to remove the top piece from the tube. The uncut front portion of the tube will be the head of the rabbit. Staple one ear on each side of the tube just behind the head.

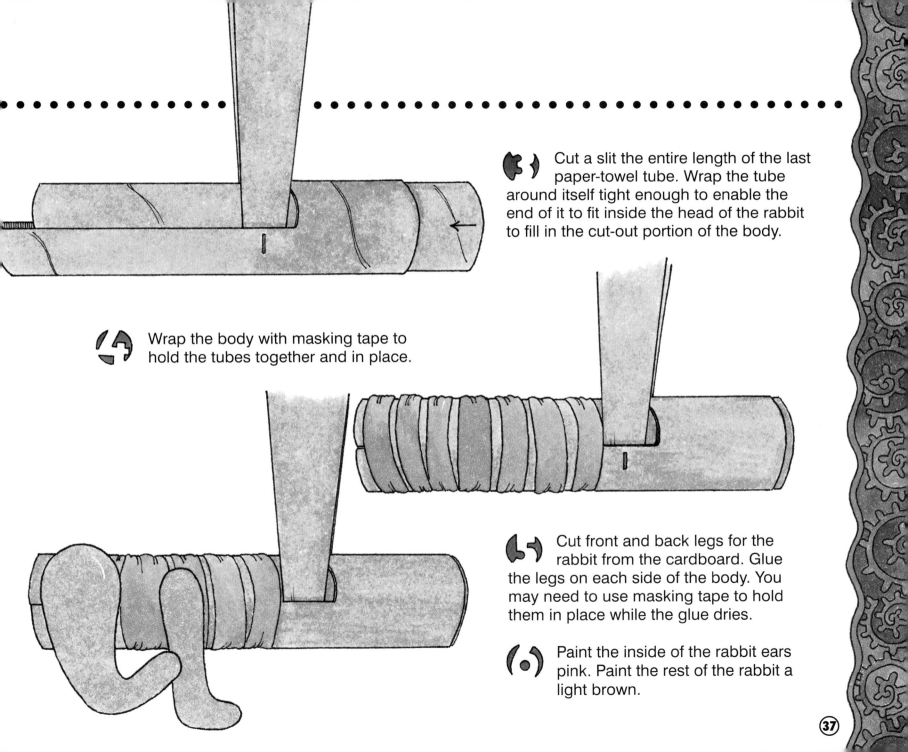

Cut a slit the entire length of the last paper-towel tube. Wrap the tube around itself tight enough to enable the end of it to fit inside the head of the rabbit to fill in the cut-out portion of the body.

Wrap the body with masking tape to hold the tubes together and in place.

Cut front and back legs for the rabbit from the cardboard. Glue the legs on each side of the body. You may need to use masking tape to hold them in place while the glue dries.

Paint the inside of the rabbit ears pink. Paint the rest of the rabbit a light brown.

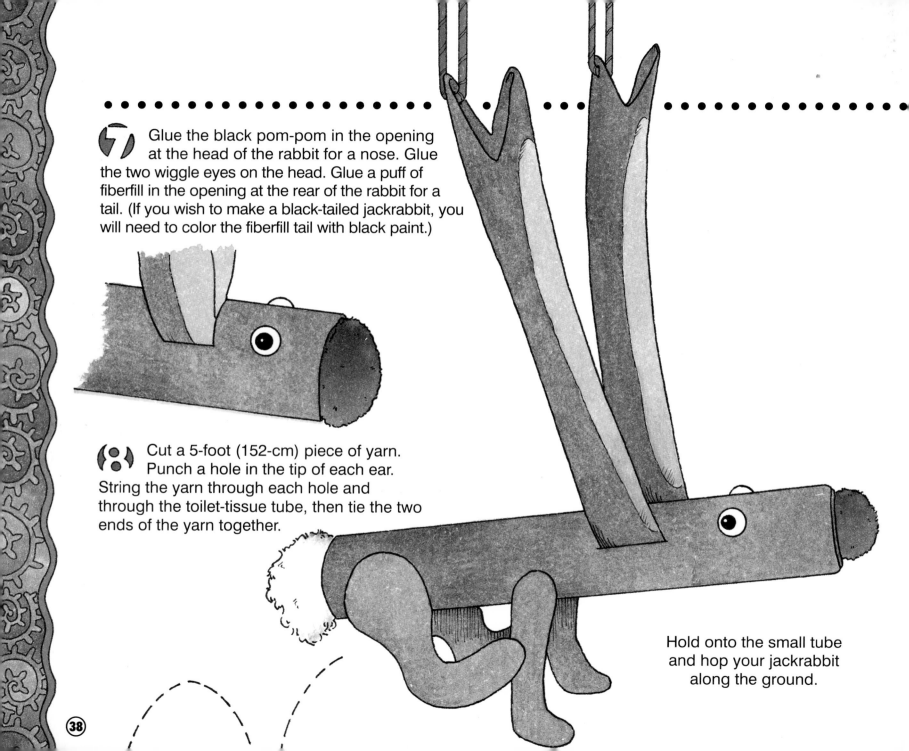

7 Glue the black pom-pom in the opening at the head of the rabbit for a nose. Glue the two wiggle eyes on the head. Glue a puff of fiberfill in the opening at the rear of the rabbit for a tail. (If you wish to make a black-tailed jackrabbit, you will need to color the fiberfill tail with black paint.)

8 Cut a 5-foot (152-cm) piece of yarn. Punch a hole in the tip of each ear. String the yarn through each hole and through the toilet-tissue tube, then tie the two ends of the yarn together.

Hold onto the small tube and hop your jackrabbit along the ground.

Envelopes Camel Puppet

Here is what you need:

brown construction paper
scissors
white glue
black marker
two identical brown greeting-card envelopes
   (you may need to color white ones)

Here is what you do:

The dromedary camel has only one hump.

Cut four legs, a tail, a head, and two ears for the camel from the brown construction paper.

Glue the two ears on the head. Draw a face for the camel with the black marker.

Open the flaps of the two envelopes. Hold the backs of the two envelopes together with the flaps open. Glue the edges of the two sides and flaps of the envelope together, leaving the bottom open. The flaps of the envelopes will form the two sides of the hump of the camel.

While the glue is still wet, slip the head between the glued envelopes on one side, and the tail on the other.

Glue a front and back leg on each side of the envelopes.

To use the camel puppet, just slip your hand between the two envelopes at the bottom and take this "ship of the desert" for a walk.

Plate Gerbil

Here is what you need:

two 9-inch (23-cm) paper plates
scissors
stapler
newspaper to work on
brown paint
paintbrush
scrap of brown construction paper
white glue
two large wiggle eyes
ruler
black thread
brown pom-pom
hole punch
6-inch (15-cm) brown pipe cleaner

Gerbils do not need to drink because they can live on the water created when their food is digested.

Here is what you do:

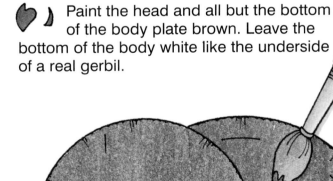

Cut a slit in one paper plate from the edge to the center of the plate. Wrap the plate partway around itself to make a cone-shaped head for the gerbil. Staple the head to one side of the second paper plate.

Paint the head and all but the bottom of the body plate brown. Leave the bottom of the body white like the underside of a real gerbil.

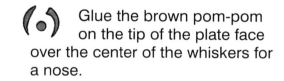

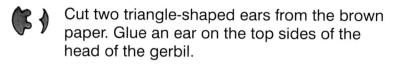 Cut two triangle-shaped ears from the brown paper. Glue an ear on the top sides of the head of the gerbil.

Glue the two wiggle eyes on the head below the ears.

Cut several 6-inch (15-cm) strands of black thread. Glue them across the point of the plate head for whiskers.

(•) Glue the brown pom-pom on the tip of the plate face over the center of the whiskers for a nose.

Punch a hole in the edge of the plate across from the head. Thread the end of the pipe cleaner through the hole for a tail, wrapping the end around itself to hold the tail in place.

Gerbils stuff the stretchy pouches in their cheeks with food to carry back to their burrows.

Coyote Paper Keeper

Here is what you need:

cereal box
scissors
newspaper to work on
yellow poster paint
paintbrush
pencil
brown construction paper
white glue
black marker

While coyotes are able to survive in a variety of climates, they are often associated with American desert areas.

Here is what you do:

 1 Cut the box into two triangle-shaped pieces by cutting from the bottom corner to the opposite corner at the top of the box. You will use the bottom triangle of the box for the body of the coyote.

2 Paint the inside of the box yellow and let it dry.

3 Trace around the two triangle sides of the box on the brown paper and cut the triangles out.

4 Trace around the bottom and the side edge of the box on the brown paper. Cut the shape out leaving about ½-inch (1 cm) of extra paper on each side of the tracing.

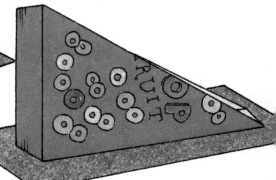

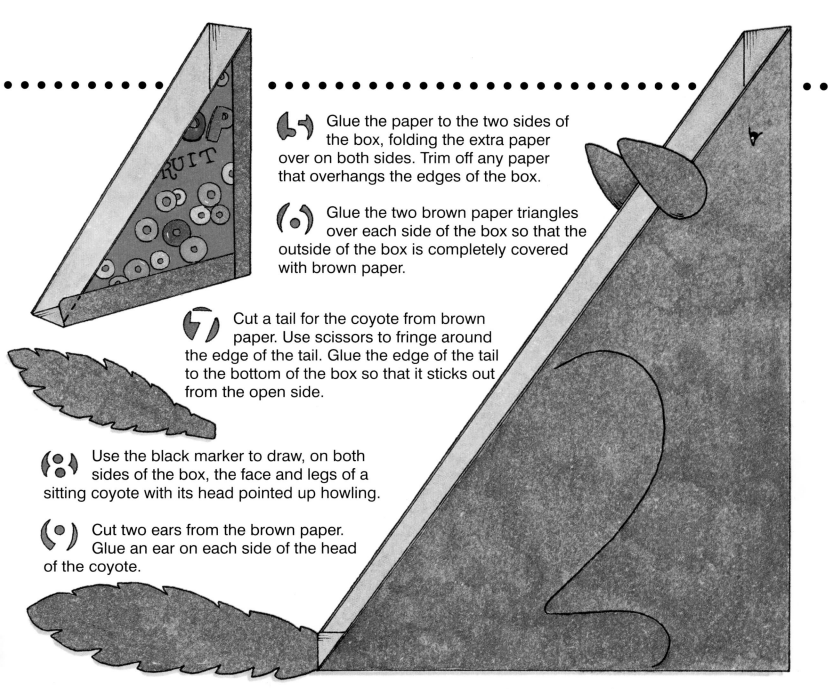

5. Glue the paper to the two sides of the box, folding the extra paper over on both sides. Trim off any paper that overhangs the edges of the box.

6. Glue the two brown paper triangles over each side of the box so that the outside of the box is completely covered with brown paper.

7. Cut a tail for the coyote from brown paper. Use scissors to fringe around the edge of the tail. Glue the edge of the tail to the bottom of the box so that it sticks out from the open side.

8. Use the black marker to draw, on both sides of the box, the face and legs of a sitting coyote with its head pointed up howling.

9. Cut two ears from the brown paper. Glue an ear on each side of the head of the coyote.

This howling coyote will be glad to sit on your desk to hold important papers and letters.

Oasis Stamp Licker

Here is what you need:

2 brown 12-inch (30-cm) pipe cleaners
2 green 12-inch (30-cm) pipe cleaners
plaster of paris mix
water
small plastic margarine tub
newspaper
blue sponge
ruler
scissors
white glue
sand

An oasis is an area of the desert that has a steady supply of water.

Here is what you do:

Make a palm tree by folding the two brown pipe cleaners in half and twisting them together to form the trunk of the tree. Use the green pipe cleaners to shape palm leaves for the tree. Slide the ends of the palm-leaves pipe cleaners through the folded end of the tree-trunk pipe cleaners to attach them.

Mix the plaster in the margarine tub according to the package directions. The tub should be about three quarters full of plaster.

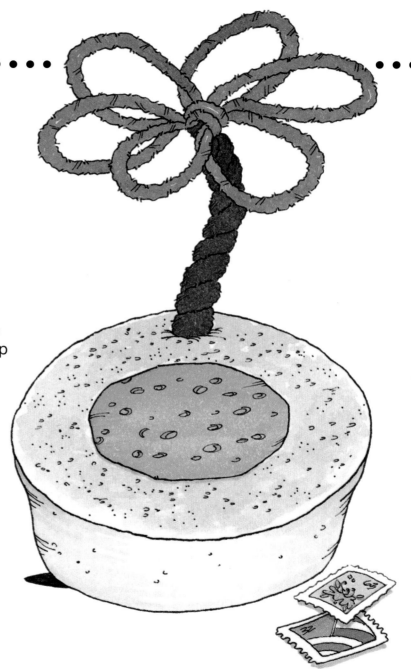

Cut a 2-inch (5-cm) circle from the blue sponge. Before the plaster has set, press the sponge into the center of the tub until the top of the sponge is level with the plaster.

Press the base of the palm tree into the wet plaster beside the sponge "water."

Let the plaster set completely, then remove the plaster shape from the tub.

Cover the top of the plaster around the sponge water with white glue, then sprinkle it with sand. Let the glue dry.

To use the oasis stamp licker just moisten the sponge with water and rub stamps across the sponge to wet them.

Sand Art Necklace

Here is what you need:

craft sand in two or more colors
clear film canister or pill bottle with a lid
masking tape
ruler
yarn
scissors
white glue
scrap of felt

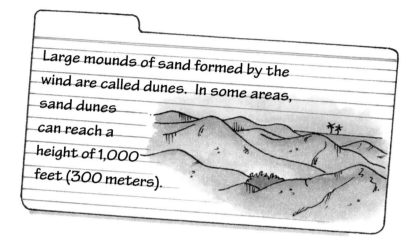

Large mounds of sand formed by the wind are called dunes. In some areas, sand dunes can reach a height of 1,000 feet (300 meters).

Here is what you do:

 Layer the colors of sand in the plastic bottle to make a pretty design. Fill the bottle to the very top, then snap the lid on to keep the layers from shifting.

Wrap the masking tape around the edge of the lid and the bottle to seal it.

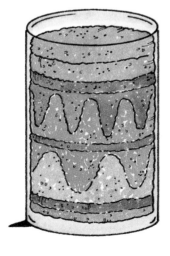
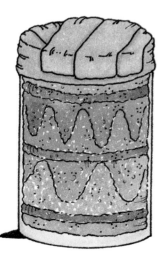

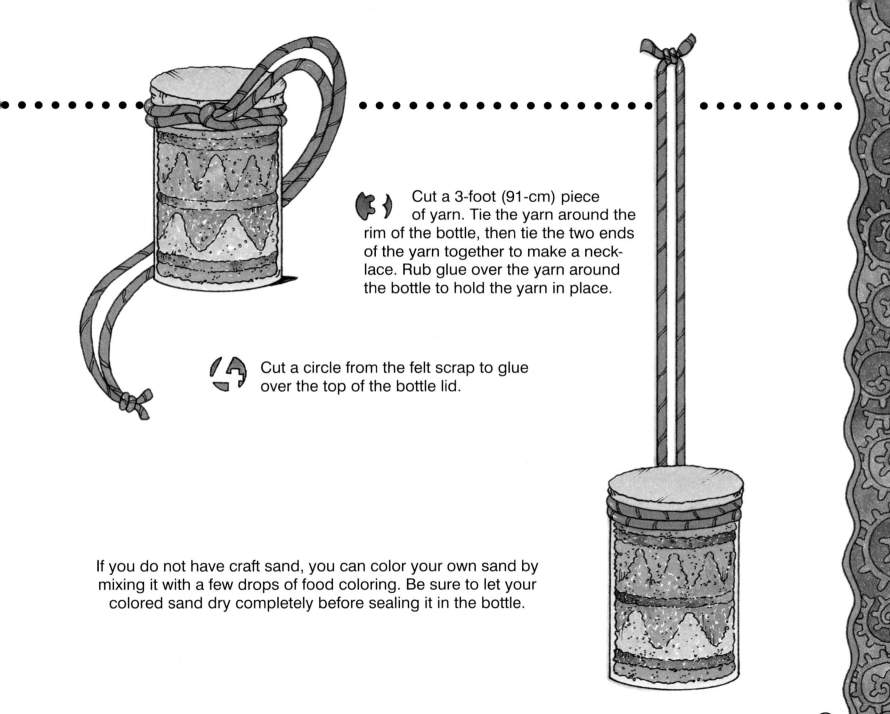

Cut a 3-foot (91-cm) piece of yarn. Tie the yarn around the rim of the bottle, then tie the two ends of the yarn together to make a necklace. Rub glue over the yarn around the bottle to hold the yarn in place.

Cut a circle from the felt scrap to glue over the top of the bottle lid.

If you do not have craft sand, you can color your own sand by mixing it with a few drops of food coloring. Be sure to let your colored sand dry completely before sealing it in the bottle.

Books About Deserts

Albert, Richard E. *Alejandro's Gift.* San Francisco: Chronicle Books, 1994.

Arnold, Caroline. *A Walk in the Desert.* Parsippany, NJ: Silver Press, 1990.

Cloudsley-Thompson, John Leonard. *Animals of the Desert.* New York: McGraw-Hill, 1971.

Flanagan, Alice. *Desert Birds.* Danbury, CT: Children's Press, 1996.

Gibson, Barbara. *Creatures of the Desert World*. Washington, D.C.: National Geographic Society, 1987.

Greenaway, Frank. *Desert Life.* New York: Dorling Kindersley, 1992.

Hirschi, Ron. *Desert.* New York: Bantam Books, 1992.

Macquity, Miranda. *Desert.* New York: Alfred A. Knopf, 1994.

Savage, Stephen. *Animals of the Desert.* Austin, TX: Raintree Steck-Vaughn Publishers, 1997.

Spencer, Guy. *A Living Desert.* Mahwah, NJ: Troll Associates, 1988.

Taylor, Bradford. *Desert Life.* London: Dorling Kindersley, 1992.

Twist, Clint. *Deserts.* New York: Dillon Press, 1991.

Wallace, Marianne D. *America's Deserts.* Golden, CO: Fulcrum Kids, 1996.

Weiwandt, Thomas. *The Hidden Life of the Desert.* New York: Crown Publishers, 1990.

Wright-Frierson, Virginia. *A Desert Scrapbook: Dawn to Dusk in the Sonoran Desert.* New York: Simon and Schuster Books for Young Readers, 1996.